Dare To Live

Devotions For
Those Over The Hill,
Not Under It!

Elizabeth Van Liere

Elizabeth Van Liere

Published by:
Christian Devotions Ministries
P.O. Box 6494
Kingsport, TN 37663
www.christiandevotions.us
books@christiandevotions.us

Published in association with
Lighthouse Publishing of the
Carolinas.

ISBN-13: 978-0-9833196-0-3

Available in print from your local
bookstore, online, or from the
publisher at:
www.christiandevotions.us
www.christiandevotionsbooks.com

Dare To Live

Churches and other non-commercial interests may reproduce portions of this book without the express written permission of Christian Devotions Ministries, provided the text does not exceed 500 words. When reproducing text from this book, include the following credit line: "From DARE TO LIVE: Devotions For Those Over The Hill, Not Under It! published by Christian Devotions Ministries. Used by permission."

Elizabeth Van Liere

Table of Contents

Should people cheat God? Yet you have cheated me! But you ask, 'What do you mean? When did we ever

And I never once complained to Israel's leaders, the shepherds of my people. I have never asked them, "Why haven't

ELizaBeTH VaN LieRe

Dedication

To the One who has been, and still is, teaching me how to live.

Introduction

We seniors are a strange lot. Getting a discount on coffee at McDonalds makes us grin, yet small changes in routine often bug us. Decisions—should I or should I not?—churn through our minds. We let worries creep into our lives so that sleep eludes us. Hopefully, the following devotions will lead the reader to lean on God, accept what disturbs, settle wayward thoughts by prayer, and send hope into the heart.

My thanks go out to the encouragement of family, good critiques by a friend, and lessons learned from the teaching of editors and authors in workshops and conferences. I especially want to thank Eddie Jones and Cindy Sproles, partners of Christian Devotions Ministries, for saying yes to the idea for these devotions, and for their help in making this book come to life.

Writing for me has been a life-long process. It is a joy, which is intensified when the writing is used to bring honor and glory to God. I hope this book may reflect this joy and bring the reader into a closer relationship with God.

Chasing After the Wind

Everything was meaningless,
a chasing after the wind.
Ecclesiastes 2:11b (NIV)

My husband retired. Then he died.

We had saved and skimped all our lives, looking forward to fun times together in the future. Now I wondered, for what? We had been chasing the wind. All our plans for doing, going, and enjoying life together had been blown away by that traitorous wind.

I was left standing there, alone.

The words of poet Robert Browning had always made me

smile in anticipation: "Grow old along with me! The best of life is yet to be, the last for which the first was made." Now I wanted to yell: "Those are stupid, meaningless words, Browning. You died young, so what did you know?"

As to the writer of Ecclesiastes, according to tradition, Solomon was wealthy, wise, and abundantly blessed with wives. Yet he felt all was meaningless, a chasing after the wind. Why? Because he was bored. Bored? I wish I'd had the chance to get bored. How could Solomon know what it was like to be lonely?

Depression hung over me like a dark cloud. Along with it came anger. A fierce anger that made me clench my fists and stomp my feet. Chet was gone and our dreams had disappeared with him.

The cloud lingered until the day

I forced myself to leave my dark thoughts behind and go outdoors. As I walked, I heard a bird sing. I looked up and found it in the newly green leaves of a huge cottonwood tree. The sky was blue as only Colorado skies can be. Billowy white clouds drifted by, touched here and there with a golden ray. My heart responded and I hurried home. I picked up a familiar book— not Browning's *Pippa Passes*—but another work filled with familiar words I knew, but had shoved aside. "I am the resurrection and the life," said the author. "He who believes in me will live, even though he dies."

In those few words I found a gift from God; a precious promise. I realized "the best of life, the last for which the first was made," was just ahead. I no longer wanted to chase after the wind.

So, when you are aching for

what is no longer yours, cling to this promise of Jesus. Look up. Smile again. Share your journey through your dark days with others whose hearts are heavy as yours once was. Help them see what you found—a brighter day is ahead. Pass on the promise you were given. It can awaken new life to those whose days are dead.

Prayer

Heavenly Father, for the many blessings you have given, especially the promise of eternal life through Jesus, thank you. Help me pass this on so others may be lifted from despair to joy. Because I love Jesus, Amen.

A Step Further

John 5:24; I John 5:11, 12

Building Blocks of Faith

Don't chase the wind. Instead, let the Spirit of God blow through you.

Questions

Do I sometimes feel I am chasing after a wind that can't be caught? Is eternal life a reality for me?

A Crown of Gray Hair

Gray hair is a crown of spender; it is attained by a righteous life.
Proverbs 16:31 (NIV)

"Gran'ma, why don't you dye your hair?" my ten-year old grandson asked with more truth than tact. "It sure is gray."

"No way," I said. "You and your three brothers are the cause of it," I said, smiling. "I earned every one of these white hairs."

The writer of Proverbs calls my pewter locks a crown of splendor. Ha! Some tiara. Every day the hair on the back of my head needs to be brushed just so, in order to cover my pink scalp. Next, my curling iron makes it look classy (I hope) and hair spray holds it all in place. All this fuss, just to make me look like someone I'm not.

My dad, uncles, and grandfather wore crowns too—fringes of silvery hair around their shiny bald heads. Their crowns were a bit lower on their heads, just above the ears as I recall, but baldness didn't bother them. What they missed in hair they made up for, talking about God and their love for Jesus whenever our family got together. Sometimes I'd stand around the corner and eavesdrop. What I heard convinced me at an early age to accept Jesus as my Savior.

But now, as I view my not-so-regal crown in the mirror, I wonder: Could my thinning gray hair reflect a woefully thin righteous relationship with God?

Surely not. When I accepted Jesus as my Savior I knew I must repent when I sin and *try* to obey God's commands. Acceptance. Repentance. Obedience. These three steps made me a child of God. Therefore, I can stop worrying, because according to His Word, He has made me righteous, thinning crown and all.

So, let's wear our gray crowns, skimpy as they may be. Let's keep them shiny clean and brush over the thinning spots where we find them. We can use a curling iron and hair spray if necessary and when we look in the mirror, let our crowns remind us of His crown of thorns and the years of love our Savior has given us.

Prayer

Heavenly Father, thank You for the people in my life who led me to You. Help me be worthy of this crown you have given me. Let it remind me to live as you want me to live, always putting You first in all I do and say. Because of Jesus, Amen.

A Step Further

Isaiah 46:4; Psalm 17:15

Building Blocks of Faith:

God looks on the inside, not the outside of a person.

Questions

What is most important, how I look to God or to other people? Can being neat and clean reflect how I feel about God?

Remember This

Bless the Lord, O my soul, and
forget not all his benefits.
Psalm 103:2 (KJ)

"Look at this, Cel. Isn't this
wonderful?" Don asked.

Cel's husband came to her
carrying his Bible. Don pointed to a
verse he had just read. Although he
was slipping into the early stages
of Alzheimer's, Don's grasp of the
Bible remained important and
comforting.

"It was such a joyous moment,"
Cel commented to me later. "I can
still see his smile as he showed me

the passage." A faraway look came into her eyes and she whispered, "I could feel God's presence with us." Her words made me hungry for the same knowledge: that God is with me.

Don's increasing memory loss brought pain to Cel and her family. Even so, shaking hands with someone while I strain my brain to think of their name makes me bite my lip to keep from laughing—until I let myself begin to worry about *my* possible memory loss.

There was a day I panicked. Oh, no! It's starting, I thought. It happened several weeks ago. My neighbor, Helen, had gone to a potluck luncheon with me. We drove to her house and as she left to go inside I said, "I'm going after my mail." I walked across the street and retrieved the mail from my box.

ELIZABETH VAN LIERE

Another neighbor wandered up with his golden retriever, and I bent down to pet his silky fur. "What a lovely dog," I said as his owner and I began walking together up the street toward our two homes. When I reached my front door I found it locked. How odd, I thought.

I rang the doorbell and my grandson answered. "Why didn't you come through the garage, Gran'ma?" He looked past me toward the empty driveway, then onto the street. "And where's your car?"

"Umm . . . just dropping off the mail." I hurried back to Helen's house where my car stood, still idling in her driveway. I sneaked a look at Helen's front window. Lucky me. She hadn't seen my goof. Within minutes I had backed out of her driveway and driven two houses down to mine. I offered my

24

grandson no explanation. Later I joked about it, telling my daughter, "Guess what I did when I went to the church potluck?"

She listened, sighed and said, "Oh, Mom." For her, that was the end of it. But not for me. For me, the incident weighed on my mind. Could it be the beginning of dementia? I wondered. Or worse? Probably just too many things on my mind, I reasoned.

We would all do well to keep our minds active. We can take a lesson from my friend Don; work hard to dig deeper into our Bible and memorize verses. (I hear such exercises help.) I hope so, because I never want to forget what Christ has done for me... even if I can't remember where I parked my car.

Prayer

Heavenly Creator, the minds you have given us are so wonderful. Help us to fill them with things worth remembering. Things like your love and forgiveness, people like your Son, Jesus, who bought salvation for us, and those special words from Your book. In Jesus' name, Amen.

A Step Further

Psalm 119:11-16; John 14:26

Building Blocks of Faith

We may forget God but He never forgets us.

Questions

Does the future scare me? What can I do about it?

26

Chocolates are Yummy but God is Sweeter

So then whether you eat or drink or whatever you may do, do all for the honor and glory of God.
I Corinthians 10:31 (Amplified)

What is the first goodie to disappear on a dessert table during the fellowship hour at church? Anything chocolate—especially brownies. Ask those among you who is a chocoholic and hands are lifted high with the enthusiasm of a praise and worship band. And happy day! I just read, "Dark chocolate is good for you." Those words help push aside my guilty feelings when I let a piece of

27

chocolate slowly melt in my mouth.

It's not so much the one piece I savor. It's when I buy a box of chocolates. Not a huge box—no more than a double layer of brown nuggets. One of my daughters-in-law can buy a Hershey's candy bar and eat one square a day. Not me. I open the box . . . slowly inhale the aroma . . . linger over the choice. Will it be a chocolate-covered caramel, a chocolate-covered truffle, or a crunchy chunk filled with nuts?

I snatch the truffle and shut the box.

Moments later the lid is off again. Just one more piece, then I'll stop.

Sin is like my addiction to chocolate. To live as God wants me to live, especially in light of His grace, requires that I develop self-control in all things — including chocolate. Paul tells us we are to glorify God at all times. This includes eating, drinking, working, or playing. "I will not be mastered by anything," Paul told the church at Corinth.

Chocolates are only one of God's gifts to us. Gobbling one piece after another means the object masters us instead of our being the master, just as overindulging in *anything* can rule our lives. God's sweetness is more important than cravings for chocolate. Do you suppose a chocolate obsession reveals a soul that is weak and easily led astray?

Prayer

Heavenly Father, You know I cannot keep my hand out of the box of chocolates by myself. I need Your help. So let my eyes skip over the sale at Walgreens for chocolates. Keep my eyes on the road ahead instead of to the side where Stouffers beckons. Grow self-control in me in everything, so all I eat, drink, or do, glorifies You. In Jesus' name, Amen.

A Step Further

Proverbs 25:16; I Corinthians 9:24-27

Building Blocks of Faith

Taste and see that the Lord is good.

Questions

Why do I feel I can indulge myself just because I'm elderly? Does it really matter if I take four pieces of candy instead of one?

You Call That Worship?

Sing a new song to the Lord! Let the whole earth sing to the Lord!
Psalm 96:1 (NLT)

Drums, guitars, and keyboard—contemporary songs with ear-splitting "noise." Sure, I sometimes ask people to repeat their words, but the clanging and banging of the worship team, mixed with the hand clapping and toe tapping, will soon leave me totally deaf. Besides that, I can't appreciate the sermon because I now have a headache. I think I'll have to wear ear plugs for the worship service. I hope this isn't what the psalmist meant when he commanded us to sing "a new song" to the Lord.

Last Sunday's worship service began with two old familiar hymns. Let me say it again: *Old, familiar hymns!* To those of us senior citizen ladies—widows—strung out in one pew, it sounded like old home week, but even smiling broadly at the worship leader to show our appreciation made no difference. It was back in full force to the contemporary "music" this week. Hmm... do you think our husbands are praising God in heaven with hymns? Or did the contemporary songs float upwards? If so, I hope I'll be better able to enjoy them there.

You don't hear too much controversy about contemporary versus traditional worship anymore. Things have settled down. We seniors lost the battle and the war, and no longer have the energy or legs to stand and fight—especially when it takes both hands for some of us to maneuver our walkers down the aisles. And it's not like we're not *trying* to like the new songs. We squint to read the words on the screen—when our failing eyesight reaches that far. We turn our hearing aids down because the beat of the drums makes us want to put our hands over our ears. Then we can't hear at all. We try to hum along when we can find a tune uncluttered with notes and chords.

Disgruntled, I once asked our minister, "Why can't we sing more hymns?"

"The newer music draws the young families," he said. "It's the kind of music they hear on the radio and TV."

How well I know. My grandkids say the hymns put them to sleep. And their most precious possessions? Their guitars, drums, and earphones.

I'll be honest. Part of my resentment toward praise and worship music is the lingering fear that *our* sometimes squeaky voices no longer count—that we oldsters are no longer important. Is it selfishness to want to be noticed, recognized, and remembered? Also, wouldn't it be good for the newer generation to learn to enjoy some of *our* songs; the ones their grandparents grew up with?

Music has changed from early chants to singing psalms to hymns, and now to contemporary songs. Maybe it's time we let the younger generation find their way to God through their music. Perhaps it's time for us (the seniors) to listen and ponder the words of the new songs, even if we can't keep up with the beat. I guess it's time for us to sing to the Lord, even if it's just in our hearts. As for me, I'll try. I really will, God.

Still, when my time comes to leave earth for heaven, it would be great if someone would hold my hand and softly sing, "Standing on the promises of Christ my King." This song will assure me of His strength when I no longer have any of my own.

Prayer

Father, there's so much to accept about change. Forgive us for wanting to stay in one place. Help us to open our minds and our hearts so others may draw closer to You. We know how blessed this relationship is and we want others to know this as well. In Jesus' name, Amen.

Elizabeth Van Liere

A Step Further

Psalm 96:1-6; Romans 12:4-8

Building Blocks of Faith

God plans every direction.
We only need to follow.

Questions

Am I stuck in my ways? Can I be gracious for the sake of young people?

Do I Look Like A Child?

To everything there is a season, a time
for every purpose under the sun.
Ecclesiastes 3:I (NKJ)

For several years I drove 325 miles to attend a yearly writers' conference in the Rocky Mountains of Colorado. Now my darling children have decided I'm too old to make the trip alone. "No more driving that far by yourself," they announced.

"Whatever for?" I asked.

"Mom, you said your reflexes just aren't that good any more."

Ugh. When will I learn to keep my

mouth shut?

So anyway, last spring my daughter drove me 125 miles to a rest stop. One of my sons picked me up there and drove another 125 miles to his brother's house in Denver. A few days later my second son took me the final 75 miles to the conference in Estes Park. I felt like a worn and weathered baton, passed from hand-to-hand. At the conclusion of the conference my daughter picked me up and hauled me home.

Hauled me home. Sounds depressing. I can picture myself in a trailer behind a semi, as if I'm cargo being shipped about. There's a fight going on inside me. Aging is like a cage, with me inside, pacing back and forth like a lion, roaring to get out and be free once more.

It seems I'm at the point where

the children (mine) have become my parents. Honestly, do I *look* like a child(gray-haired,wearingpolyester pants suits, and Reebok walking shoes)? I'm not even allowed to get things from a top cupboard by standing on a stepstool. "Don't want you to fall," they say. Hey, I've fallen before...for their dad when he was courting me and *that* didn't hurt. But I understand their concern— to a point. Friends *have* fallen and broken a hip or leg and I'd hate to inflict extra care on my kids.

When I grumbled to my friends about my bossy kids reigning me in, did I get any sympathy? No. My complaints fell on... (drum roll, please) deaf ears. "Your kids care about you," a friend said.

Sure, I understand . . . kind of. But flowers or a box of chocolates (even better) would warm my heart even more. Just *please* don't take away my driving privileges.

I used to love taking long drives by myself. The car radio would be turned up loud with some of Vivaldi's classical music, matching the mountain scenery. A sense of freedom. A time to worship God in solitude and admire the majesty of his creation. To think about the articles I hoped to have critiqued at the workshops and a time to pray about the conference. All that changed when I was *driven* instead of *driving.*

Is this what Solomon meant when he said, "There is a time for everything?"

When we're young, we're "driven" to succeed, conquer, and build. Now I'm being "driven" to let go and let others do for me. Losing the privilege of driving means I can no longer control where and when and how I go. It looks as though I'm out of control of my destiny.

But really, I recognize we (me included) were never in control of our destiny. I've heard people say, "God is my co-pilot." Wrong. He is the *pilot,* whether we know it or not. He is the one who has been in control of our lives all these years. It's time to acknowledge this and say, "Okay, God. Take over."

Do I look like a child? Indeed I do—a child of the King.

Prayer

Heavenly Father, help me accept this gracefully. Help me, the parent, become the child. And thank you, God, for loving me so much you gave me children who care for me when so many people do not have that joy. In Jesus' name, Amen.

A Step Further

Psalm 25:4-6; Ecclesiastes 5:19, 20

Building Blocks of Faith

If God is your pilot, then you're
safe in the passenger seat.

Questions

Can I relax and let my children
care for me? How can I show them I
appreciate it instead of grumbling?

Hey Dude, Stop Hitting on Me!

....A time to weep and a time to laugh; A time to mourn and a time to dance.
Ecclesiastes 3:4 (NAS)

The call came from Telluride, 65 miles south of Montrose. "Mrs. Van Liere, my dad lives in Pennsylvania. He read something in a booklet you had written and it touched him. He noticed you live in Montrose and asked me to call you to see if he could write you."

Be careful, I thought, and asked, "Is this a scam?"

"No ma'am, it's not a scam," the

man on the other end of the phone said. He chuckled and said, "my dad only wants to get in touch with you." I gave him my address and within a week I received a letter from Fred. I replied with a thank you. Fred wrote again, and again … and yet again. What have I begun? I wondered. Whatever it was grew into his visit to my Sunday morning Bible study a few months later.

He popped into the class as though he had been coming a long time. "Is Betty Van Liere here?" he asked.

In front of a grinning group of seniors I said, "Yup. That's me."

He sat down next to me, put his arm around the back of my chair, fit right into the study, and asked me out to lunch after church. Over Chinese food we told each other about our deceased spouses, our kids, and our grandkids. Three hours later his son and daughter-in-law picked him up. The following Sunday he showed up again for another *visit.* That Monday he flew back to Pennsylvania. I'll admit I enjoyed our *dates.*

Each Sunday afternoon he called and we talked a little while. As a widow of almost twenty years I suddenly felt younger. But then Valentine's Day came and he surprised me with a lovely bouquet of flowers…and an overly friendly note.

It had been fun, but after years of no man around I was used to doing *what* I wanted to do, *when* I wanted to do it. And one thing I do not want is to have strings attached. I called him on the phone. "Fred, you're movin' too fast. Please don't get serious," I said.

He replied: "At our age, moving at all is cause for celebration, but no problem. We can just be friends."

I sighed in relief...until he sent an up-beat clipping his daughter mailed him about seniors dating. Next I learned he had made plane reservations to come for a week in June—to Montrose, not Telluride.

My friends said, "Great!" My daughter frowned. One of my sons announced: "I ain't callin' him Dad." (Don't worry, Ryan. Nothing's gonna' happen.)

Solomon says there is a time for everything. *A time to mourn and a time to dance...*I do know Fred attends dances in his home town. It's been ages since I danced, so I'd probably clump all over his feet. Still, I'm willing to try again. But like my widowed mother-in-law once said when she was approached by a neighbor to go out for coffee, "I'm gonna hang a sign around my neck: Not for rent and not for sale."

Don't get me wrong. Fred may not be Mr. Right *for me*, but he is a really nice person. He holds my hand and tells me he cares. It's good for us to know we can still be important to someone besides our family. When this happens, it's up to us to accept it as an unexpected blessing from God.

Prayer

Heavenly Father, you've sent someone into my life who is bringing an added smile to my face. Help me enjoy this fun blessing. In Jesus' Name, Amen.

ELɪZᴀʙᴇᴛʜ Vᴀɴ Lɪᴇʀᴇ

A Step Further

Genesis 2:18; Ecclesiastes 4:9-10
(verse 11—if dating leads to
marriage)

Building Blocks of Faith

God loves to send blessings into
our lives. It's up to us to accept
them or reject them.

Questions

Do I want dating to become
serious? How can I keep from
hurting the other person?

Looks Can Be Deceiving

Abstain from all appearance of evil.
I Thessalonians 5:22 (King James)

The day arrived. With it came Fred, and a silent nervous prayer from me: "Lord, please show me where to go with Fred and what to do. This could be a long week."

Fred checked into a motel, received two keys, and handed one to me.

"What do I need this for?" I asked.

"So you can come on in if I'm not ready."

"Oh . . .uh . . .well . . . okay," I said, slipping the plastic key into my

49

purse.

Later I casually mentioned Fred's comment to my daughter. She relayed the message to my son. He called and I heard the bomb blast from 250 miles away. "Mother, he says he's a Christian. Why would he want you coming into his room when he's not dressed?"

His comment floored me. "Ryan! We're in our eighties. I'm sure he didn't mean anything by it."

Why were my kids making such a big deal about something as small as a key? So what if I'd go into his room and wait while he took a shower? Big deal. I'd turn on the TV and relax. Fred would come out (fully dressed) and we'd go for dinner. It wasn't like we were high schoolers catching a motel room after the prom.

Nor was it like I was going on

the road with Fred. My friend in Minnesota took several trips with her male friend, with the two of them sleeping in his travel-trailer. And another acquaintance of mine moved in with her male friend. He gave her a place to live when the assisted living place bled her savings dry. All Fred did was give me an extra key. Why had I even mentioned it? Guess I should have given the dumb key back to Fred.

Meanwhile, I explained to my son. "I didn't intend to *use* the key," I said. "I meant to knock on the door."

"But think of how it looks, Mom."

I couldn't help but laugh. Such a to-do about nothing. Then I thought about my granddaughters. I could guess what they might say. "Gran'ma was in some guy's motel room while he was taking a shower. If *she* wasn't bothered by hanging out in some man's room…"

I filled in the rest and cringed.

Guess Ryan was right. I see how the look of questionable behavior can touch others and make them think it's okay. And that makes it doubly wrong. Perhaps that's why scripture tells us to abstain from all appearances of indecency. I never intended to *use* the key, but I should have been more careful in the signals I sent to my children… and to Fred. The "key" to righteous living is doing right in God's eyes every time—and especially for others who are watching.

Prayer

Heavenly Judge, You established right from wrong from the very beginning and put this knowledge in our hearts. Keep me from leading anyone astray, I pray. In Jesus' loving Name, Amen.

A Step Further

Malachi 3:6,7; Matthew 18:6,7

Building Blocks of Faith

Wisdom comes with age and an old fool is still a fool.

Questions

Am I following today's ways instead of God's ways? Although I'm older, am I wiser?

Pass It On

You have been treated generously,
so live generously.
Matthew 10:8b (The Message)

When Leonard and Ella got engaged, he told her: "I have a surprise for you." He hitched his horse to a buggy, helped Ella inside, and off they went. Several miles later, down a bumpy road, they pulled up to a white, two-story house. "Like it?" he asked. "I bought it for us."

Her excited smile told him, yes!

Leonard and Ella conceived my husband in that house and twenty years later, became my in-laws. Leonard never owned a credit card. He paid for everything with his earnings, including that house he bought. My husband caught this thrifty habit from his father.

Like Dad Van Liere, my dad worked hard to support his family. Sometimes he borrowed, sometimes he lent. Oftentimes he gave. But always he dreamed.

Like my dad, I'm a dreamer with a soft heart. I live comfortably now. Thanks to my husband's frugal ways I have no need to borrow from anyone. I can even pass on the blessings God has indirectly given me.

Sometimes I give in small ways. "I have a job interview but I'm low on gas," my grandson will say.

"My lawn needs mowing," I say. My lawn gets mowed—I'm happy. My grandson helps his grandma and he doesn't feel like a charity case.

Another grandson calls to say he has a car payment due. This time the "loan" is bigger. He's out of work so, again, I help out. "Thank you, Gran'ma," he says. "I'll pay it back, but it'll be just a little at a time."

It puts a smile on my face to hear his thanks. And maybe I make God smile when I say "Thank you, God, for the blessings I have received, enabling me to help my kids."

My boys need more than money. They need to know their worth as men and that comes through hard work, earning your keep, and helping others, so I'm careful to remind them: "When you see someone in need, help. Always remember the times others have helped you and pass along the gift of giving."

Prayer

Heavenly Father, I have so much because You have given it to me. I know it's there for me to share. Help me always to be happy to pass it on. For Jesus' sake, Amen.

A Step Further

Luke 6:34-36, 38; I Timothy 6:17, 18

Building Blocks of Faith

Blessings are meant to be shared.

Questions

Am I being wise in my giving? Should I write a contract when loaning money to family?

Cheating God

Should people cheat God? Yet
you have cheated me! But you
ask, 'What do you mean? When
did we ever cheat you?' You have
cheated me of the tithes
and offerings due me.
Malachi 3:8 (NLT)

"I've never tithed," a friend
declared. "I don't dare. I may need
that extra 10% one of these days."

I understand that sort of thinking.
We seniors rely on past earnings
to pay a monthly mortgage.
Taxes come due. Utility bills keep
increasing. Food prices go up and
the return on our investments goes

down. Grandpa Van Liere once said, "I have enough clothes to last the rest of my life." True for most of us as we grow older, but even the basics, like socks and underwear, continue to rise in price.

The funny thing is, people our age skimp in some areas but not in meals. We enjoy eating out. It's *our* generation's social network. We pay for meals, often tipping 15% or even 20% to the server. If we feel, as my friend does, that we may need that extra 10% one of these days, why do we freely give it to man while skimping on God?

I began tithing soon after I found Jesus. My husband and I continued tithing after we married. We never felt short-changed. In fact, our experience confirmed Malachi's words when he spoke on behalf of God, saying: "I will open the windows of heaven for you. I will pour out a blessing so great you won't have enough room to take it in! Try it! Let me prove it to you!"

Does God still require tithing as He did in the Old Testament or are we to follow Jesus' admonition to give to Caesar what is Caesar's and give God what is God's? If I follow that line of logic, then every breath I breathe is God's, every opportunity is His, every idea, relationship, and talent I possess is His. Even the government has given me nothing that was not given to it by God. We say we are "one nation under God." Our coinage boasts, "In God we trust."

Well, do we? Do I?

Have I been able to keep up with bills and higher prices? Yes. Has God opened heaven's storehouse of blessings and filled me again and again? You bet. My limited income has never run out.

But that's not the reason I tithe. I tithe because God has given me so much more than money. He has promised me a life with Him for eternity. My small 10% may not be much in the vastness of His Kingdom, but to give back to God at all is an honor and something I will always treasure.

Prayer

Heavenly Father, the more I give to others in Your name, the more my needs are met. Let me never hold back, God, because it is all Yours in the first place. Thank You for all You've given me, especially for Jesus, who gave Himself that we might have the most wonderful gift of all, eternal life. Amen.

A Step Further

Psalms 50:9-12; Matthew 22:15-22

Building Blocks of Faith

My limited income is unlimited when filtered through His hands.

Questions

How much am I willing to give back to God? Do I understand all I have is the Lord's and is only on loan to me?

Getting My Money's Worth

Don't be obsessed with getting more material things. Be relaxed with what you have.
Hebrews 13:5a (The Message)

Spring had sprung and colorful yard sales were blooming everywhere. My car automatically came to a stop when I saw a red-lettered yard sale sign tacked to a telephone pole. I'm not stingy, but like most seniors, my hand holds firmly to my hard-earned money, so yard sales are like 4th of July rockets exploding. Their bargains draw me like a magnet.

The lavender blouse I bought for a mere $2.50, however, caused me to re-think my priorities. It looked brand-new, but at home I found two of the six buttons were missing. I went to town the next day and bought a card of similar buttons at the Dollar Store. Another dollar. I took the remaining four buttons off and sewed all six new buttons on, put the blouse on and ... oh, no . . . the buttons were too big and wouldn't go through the buttonholes. I took those buttons off and went back downtown the next day for smaller buttons. Another dollar. Changed buttons again. Finally done. Tried the blouse on and, wouldn't you know it? My $4.50 blouse was too tight. (There's no exchange on figures.)

Now I love to get my money's worth, but I surely wasted it that day by buying something I didn't need in the first place. It's another addiction; buy something because it's marked down, not because I especially want it, but because the price seems right.

I certainly did *not* get my money's worth on that blouse, but I did strike a bargain when I accepted Christ as my Savior. Through it, I obtained eternal life. No yard sale involved. No money exchanged. No bargaining. And it's free to anyone. All it takes is saying yes to Jesus.

Prayer

God, it is You who has blessed me with more than enough. Help me put my money to better use than buying things I do not need. Instead, let me open my purse to homeless people and to those without enough clothes or food. I pray in the name of Jesus, who has given so much. Amen.

Eᴌɪᴢᴀʙᴇᴛʜ Vᴀɴ Lɪᴇʀᴇ

A Step Further

Luke 12:22-34

Building Blocks of Faith

Looking for a good deal? Try God.

Questions

There are so many petitions for donations. Which ones are trustworthy? Also, do I spend time foolishly as well as money?

Digital Deity

Come and see what God has
done, how awesome His works in
man's behalf.
Psalm 66:5 (NIV)

Oh no, not again. "Doug!" I
hollered.

My grandson strolled into my
room. "Now what'd you break,
Gran'ma?"

"I didn't break anything," I
blustered. "This stupid computer
doesn't like me. I was working on a
letter and everything disappeared.
The whole computer went blank."

Doug rolled his eyes, took my

place in the chair, and ran his hands over a few keys. Magically, my letter reappeared. "You pushed the wrong button," he said, tapping the keyboard.

"You wait. One of these days I'll figure this ornery thing out myself."

"Ha!" Doug said.

Well, why should he believe me? I'm as lost in the technical world as I would be wandering through a dark forest. Occasionally I surprise the boys. For example, I ordered a book for Doug's brother through Amazon. When I gave it to Mike, he raised his eyebrows. "You ordered this yourself? With a *computer*?"

"Well, yeah. You think I'm too old and ignorant to figure it out?"

"No, of course not." But his grin didn't match his words.

Computers, cell phones, universal

remotes, 2000 channel TV cable boxes, digital cameras, digital music players, digital coffee makers ... digital anything—all exist to make my life difficult. I forget to turn my cell phone on. I forget to turn it off. I forget to charge it. I forget to plug in the charger. Ah, me. Life was easier way back when. Nevertheless, God has given me a brain, so I'll keep on using it and try my best to catch up to today's technology.

Much easier is my stand-by—my Bible. It may come in new, easier-to-read versions, but the message inside, like God Himself, doesn't change. It's always booted up, needs no batteries, and works every time. God's Word is universal (open it and read), comes in multiple language translations and has been rigorously tested by millions of users over the past centuries. True,

God is a digital God. He has done some awesome works during my lifetime but none compare to the Bible.

That's a piece of hardware I'll take with me to the grave.

Prayer

Creator God, what a wonderful world You have given us. Creation shouts of Your touch. I pray I will keep learning until You call me home. Help me use this knowledge for Your glory. In Jesus' Name, Amen.

A Step Further

Job 9:10; Psalm 145:3-6

Dare To Live

Building Blocks of Faith

The Bible: Suitable for any age group—but it is worthless if it doesn't get opened.

Questions

What gifts has God given me? What is the best way for me to use those gifts?

Quit Your Bellyaching

Therefore, strengthen the hands that are weak and the knees that are feeble, and make straight paths for your feet, so that the limb which is lame may not be put out of joint, but rather be healed.
Hebrews 12:12, 13 (NAS)

Every so often I realize I'm in an unfamiliar body. Like today—I almost looked over my shoulder to see if the real me was standing behind me. It was the doctor's fault.

"Walk," the doctor said. "Every day; fifteen minutes at a minimum."

Easy for him to say. He's still young enough to have the original parts that came with his model. Not like my friends. Many of them have plastic hips, titanium pins, and hearts aflutter with artificial valves. I know I'm getting old, but sometimes I miss the good old days when a "stint" was that short period of time your hubby served in the military.

The doctor had more good news. "Cut back on pasta, bread, and potatoes."

No problem. I can hardly taste anything anyway.

Then, as if he hadn't depressed me enough, he added, "And no rich desserts." He was kidding, right? Who can afford anything rich on my fixed income?

"You mean no chocolate cake or brownies?" I said, with my mouth already watering.

Without looking up from the chart

he nodded. "Uh huh."

"So I'm not supposed to enjoy life anymore, right?"

"How can you enjoy life if you're dead?" he replied, closing my folder. "Look, Mrs. Van Liere. The older you get the greater your chances are of developing diabetes. It's best if you cut back now before it's too late."

Too late? At the speed I'm moving, I'd have to sprint to reach too late.

What's next? I wondered. He already has me inhaling extra oxygen at night. That thing-a-ma-jig throws off so much heat I feel like I'm suffocating. I thought about mentioning to him the heartburn I get from Mexican chicken enchiladas, but decided against it. As long as the Tums are working, why risk losing another excuse for enjoying the spice of life?

All this talk of cutting-back and cutting-out left me in a sour mood, with no help from my sarcastic daughter. "You want some cheese with your whine?" she asked.

My sister-in-law's call shoved the whining aside. "I've been in pain the last couple of years, so I finally broke down and had knee surgery," she said. "Now I've started therapy and it's no fun."

After we hung up, I prayed for her healing and added: "Thank you, God, that my knees still hold me up so I *can* walk without pain."

Moments later the daughter of a close friend called. "Mom's in the hospital. She had a heart attack."

I said I'd pray and I meant it. Again, I added a "thank you, God, for my heart. It's running smoothly for the moment."

That evening I thought of my friends and their deteriorating condition and I began to cry. My tiny grievances melted away and once more I prayed. "I'm sorry for the pity-party, God. Please forgive me."

When I studied the verse in Hebrews, I heard God say: "Stop whining, strengthen your feeble arms, weak knees, and walk." And wasn't that what the doctor said to me? "Sit up, shape up, and shut up."

"Be grateful you can walk," I heard God say. And I was.

And am.

So I *will* walk. I *will* cut out unhealthy snacks. I *will* even throw off the blankets, open the windows to let the heat flow, and give thanks to God for every oxygen-enriched breath I receive. By far, the most difficult at our delicious senior potlucks, I'll try to turn away from chocolate cake or brownies. I'll need God's help for that.

Next week I see the optometrist. At least I hope to see him. Given my failing eyesight, he may send me home with a service dog. If so, the first command I'll teach the mutt will be, "walk!"

Prayer

Heavenly Father, giver of all good gifts, help me be grateful for the health I have. Help me stick to my resolves. Also, help me use my health to help others that I may glorify You. In Jesus' name, Amen.

A Step Further

Lamentations 3:21-26; Psalm 84:5-7

Building Blocks of Faith

Though our bodies are dying, our spirits are being renewed every day.

Questions

Why am I so healthy and yet so quick to complain? How can I develop a taste for healthier foods?

Rejoicing Versus Tears

Rejoice with them who do rejoice,
and weep with them that weep.
Romans 12:15 (KJ)

My friend, Cel, began therapy a month or so after her stroke. She worked through rehab but a second stroke put her back in intensive care again. Between the two strokes, her husband, Don, died.

During her married life, Cel experienced a baby's crib-death, a too-early marriage for a daughter, the divorce of a grandchild, her husband's descent into Alzheimer's, and finally, his death. Like an exclamation point to her tragic past, Cel now lies in a coma.

We often hear, "God won't give you more than you can handle," but this passage is usually misquoted. Paul was speaking in terms of temptations, not tragedy. Nonetheless, Cel and Don must have been strong people for God to allow all this heartache in one lifetime. He knew their love for Him would shine into the lives of others, even through the trials.

Cel has been an inspiration to me as long as we have been friends—over fifty years. Her gentleness and kindness are evidence of her fruitful spirit. If Cel doesn't recover from this stroke, I will rejoice.

"Rejoice if she dies?" you ask. Of course. How can we keep from rejoicing when someone goes to be with Jesus in heaven? We Christians know we will see those again who are with the Lord. But, if we do not know Jesus, the believing life of the friend or relative who loved Him can stir a desire in our hearts to find the salvation they knew.

I'll cry long and hard if Cel dies. Not because of my loss, but because of her leaving without me. I will also mourn because her family will miss her prayers for them, her sweet smile, and the love with which she showered them. But I'll also rejoice, knowing we will be reunited in Him. And on the days when I miss her the most, I'll remember the example she set of a life well lived for Him.

Prayer

God, thank You for this person who has been such a wonderful friend. Thank You for her sharing her love for You. I always felt Your presence when I met with her. Please help me be such a witness to my friends. Be with her family, Lord, and lead them on the path that Cel followed. In Jesus' Name, Amen.

A Step Further

Proverbs 17:17a; John 15:12-17

Building Blocks of Faith

The legacy we leave is based upon the lives we touched.

Questions

Am I the kind of friend who will be missed? What can I learn from Jesus about being a friend?

Thy Will or My Will

Don't act thoughtlessly, but try to
understand what the Lord wants
you to do.
Ephesians 5:17 (NLT)

"Thy will be done and *my* will be
done, do not match," my friend
Charlene said bitterly. "I prayed for
Tom to get well when he was sick,
but God let Tom die instead."

Charlene thought her will was
aligned with God's. Like railroad
tracks seeming to meet in the
distance, she thought she knew
God's mind on the matter of Tom's
health, but she didn't. Though close,
the two lines never met, leaving

Charlene shocked when Tom died. "I really believed he would get better," she exclaimed.

Now Tom's "better" is Charlene's bitterness.

I think of another friend whose will didn't match God's. The difference came when He said, "Your will, not mine, be done." God didn't remove His suffering and my friend died an excruciating death, spending His last hours gasping for breath. Why would God demand such suffering? I wondered. Especially of a man as sweet as my friend.

These dark thoughts haunt me when I pray for a loved one to be healed, a wayward child to repent, or the martyrs in other countries to be rescued, and nothing changes. Is this sadness also God's will? Can He make good come out of the hurt, disappointment, and tears?

I may have gained some wisdom as the years rolled by, but I still can't answer the question of "Why, God?" I only know He's sovereign, all-powerful, and full of love, so I am assured that in the large scheme of things He knows best.

As for my friend, the one who drowned when His lungs filled with water, I understand. He's fine now; made a complete recovery, and is seated by His Father in heaven.

Hopefully, in all the days left to me, I'll say with Jesus, "Not my will, but yours, God."

God's will. Not mine. Just His.

Prayer

Most Holy Father, who are we to ask "why" when things do not go as we wish? If we would ask, "if it is Your will" before we pray for healing, for a job, for a trip, for our children, we would be free from worry. Help me to love You so much that I am willing to always remember Your will, not mine, be done. In the Name of Jesus, who showed us how to live and how to die, Amen.

A Step Further

John 6:40; Hebrews 10:5-7; James 4:13-15

Building Blocks of Faith

Where there's God's will, there's a way out.

Questions

Am I ready to leave everything up to God? How can I make my will agree with God's?

Lord, Why Am I Still Here?

The effective prayer of a righteous
man, can accomplish much.
James 5:16b (NAS)

Remember about fifty or sixty
years ago promising to care for your
new spouse in sickness as well as in
health? Through ten tough years
of caring for her sick husband, Joe,
Mary learned what "in sickness"
meant.

The latest tests showed Joe had
congestive heart failure. He took
pills which kept him alive, but they
made him miserable and changed
his personality from nice to nasty.

The doctor said, "If you like, we can discontinue them."

Joe said, "No, I'm not ready to go. I'll continue with the pills."

Mary and Joe's daughter both knew Joe had wandered from Jesus and it broke their hearts. Every day they talked about Jesus with him and prayed together. To their joy, God's love captured him and he said "yes" again to the Lord.

Immediately afterwards Joe said, "Get the doctor for me."

When the doctor came Joe said, "Now I'm ready. Discontinue the pills." A month later he died.

Twenty years ago my believing husband also died. At least eight of my close friends have gone to heaven ahead of me. Sometimes I've wondered why I'm still here.

Moses had a purpose: to lead

God's people to the Promised Land. When he'd fulfilled that goal he died. Sampson had a purpose: to slay the enemies of God. When he did, he died. Jesus had a purpose: to die that we might live with God. He fulfilled His purpose. He died, rose again, and waits for us in heaven.

Do you wonder why you're still here? Do you suppose the reason may be something as simple but important as praying for friends and family who are still without His salvation?

The words, "the effective prayer of a righteous man can accomplish much," once made me laugh. Me? Righteous? How could I pray for anyone?

I learned righteousness is a gift God gave me when I became a forgiven sinner. Wow! What a blessing it is to know my prayers are effective and powerful. Even if I should come to the point of being unable to move my hands, legs, or lips, I'll still be able to pray and make a difference in the lives of others.

Hearing Joe's story gives me hope and reminds me I still have a reason to live: For Him…and others. We may never know the results of our prayers, but God does and that is what counts.

Prayer

God of the lost, I pray for all those who need to know of Your great love for them. Help me not only to pray, but to speak about You to those You put in my path. Thank You for saving me through the blood of Jesus, my Savior. Amen.

Elizabeth Van Liere

A Step Further

Romans 3:21-24; James 4:16a

Building Blocks of Faith

Satan won't get any bigger, but you can. Be big and bold for God.

Questions

What can I do to show my thanks for making me righteous? Is there someone who especially needs my prayers?

Time's A-Wasting

No eye has seen any God besides
you, who acts on behalf of those
who wait for Him.
Isaiah 64:4b (NIV)

I rolled over and looked at the
clock. 5 A.M. Rolled over again.
And once more. Finally gave up
and read until seven. Later, at
breakfast, I yawned and said to my
daughter, "I'm tired. I was just lying
there, waiting for morning, wasting
time, so I thought I might as well
read."

She grinned. "At your age you don't
have much time left to waste." Nice.
Next time I'm looking for comfort I'll

know who *not* to turn to.

When sleep evades me, praying for others helps. But sometimes, like the disciples in the garden, I fall back to sleep and find myself haunted by my Lord's words: "Couldn't you stay awake for just…"

Other times my thoughts wander away from whom or what I was praying for. My mind fills up with things: Clean the closet, discard unused items, or write a note to a friend whose husband just died.

Dawn finally peeks into my window. 6 A.M. I yawn, turn over, and drift off to sleep.

The next sound I hear is my daughter's shower running. 7:30 A.M. I push myself up and ease out of bed, then eat cold cereal, drink hot coffee, swallow down one-a-day vitamins, fish oil, calcium, aspirin, and the prescription drugs needed to keep me going at top speed. Then I'm ready to work my way through the list of things that filled my mind and kept me awake.

But before I do, I start with my morning dose of God's Word. Today it's from Isaiah 26.

Whoa. What's this? Verse 3 tells me to look at God, to trust in Him. It's as though God is saying, "You may be standing on the threshold of old age, but you need not rush to do more and more. Do what you can. I'll do the rest."

When I trust in me, I become frustrated. When I trust in God, the necessary things get done. Things like: Writing notes, making calls, and cleaning out closets. Often it's hard to wait on God but when I do, I feel myself relax. Must be His perfect peace; the sort of calm that leads to a peaceful night's rest after a full day of serving Him by praying, serving, and waiting on others.

Prayer

Restorer of my soul, slow me down, I pray. Keep me from being so anxious, trying to do all I did when I was younger. Help me follow the better way—your way. In the precious name of the only Way, Jesus, Amen.

A Step Further

Psalm 37:3-7; Isaiah 30:15

Building Blocks of Faith

"Rest in me," God says. "I'll do the rest."

Questions

How often do I run ahead of God? Do I trust Him enough to relax and let Him lead me?

Dare To Live!

Don't live carelessly, unthinkingly.
Make sure you understand what
the Master wants.
Ephesians 5:15 (The Message)

Chills ran down my back. I stared at two pictures of my twenty-year-old granddaughter and her husband. In one, Marcia was plastered against the sky, her mouth wide open with excitement. I almost screamed with her—in fear. I saw the huge buckles that belted her to the instructor, but the clouds behind her told me she was sky-high—and loving it.

The other photo showed her brave husband. Like Marcia, Dale's arms stuck out like a bird's wings. If his picture had come with sound, I'm sure I'd have heard a big "Yahoo!"

Foolish, foolish kids, I thought. Jumping from a plane to go skydiving! My hands grew clammy just thinking about it.

But wait. Was I hiding a touch of envy in my attitude? Wishing I was young and daring once again? Years ago I let myself get pulled up into the sky, towed by a rope behind a speeding motorboat. Legs extended as though frozen in space, hands clenching the ropes, body stiff in terror, I soared above the Sea of Cortez. I was 54-years-old— about thirty years more "grown-up" than my grandkids.

Later I heard about a man who had crashed into the water and broken his leg when the boat had slowed down and gravity took over. A sobering thought had hit me: It could have happened to me. Would the thrill of the ride have been worth the fall? Treat gravity with respect, I thought. It can pull you down.

Life offers us many risks: Dares to fulfill, blood-rushing excitement, all-for-the-fun-of-it, for the wow-I-really-did-it feeling. Is it sinful to skydive, para-sail, or ride a motorcycle for the thrill? That's like saying it's sinful to be young.

Yet, as I grow older (and I hope wiser) I find there are other boundaries to push—a different risk to take. Not for myself, however, but for Jesus.

What risk? Losing irreverent friends when I step away from their coarse jokes. Alienating a grandson when I gently mention that living with his companion outside of marriage is sinful. Being snubbed because I'm a Christian and excluded from certain gatherings. Risky business, yes, but worth the dare to live and love as Jesus did.

Accept grace with respect. It can lift you up. It comes through Jesus who offers an abundant life. So let's grab all the life we can, regardless of our age. Especially, throw caution to the wind, dare to live, and love the God who made the heavens and earth, gravity, and grace. You just may find the thrill of His joy leaves you wide-eyed and speechless.

Prayer

As a child listens to a father, so may I listen to You, my Heavenly Father. Thank You for the challenges and the fun things in life, but guide me, God, so that

Elizabeth Van Liere

whatever I do may bring You honor and glory. In Jesus' name, Amen.

A Step Further

Ephesians 4:21-24; 5:15

Building Blocks of Faith

Abundant life is available through Jesus.

Questions

What do I need in order to live as Jesus did? List the ways you glorify God with your actions.

Makeover Extreme:
The House of God

And I never once complained to
Israel's leaders, the shepherds of
my people. I have never asked
them, "Why haven't you built me a
beautiful cedar temple?"
I Chronicles 17:6 (NLT)

Have I been wrong all these
years? Going to church—a
building—on Sundays, entering the
sanctuary to worship God, filled me
with reverence. I wore a nice dress
and white gloves, along with a hat,
stockings, and dress shoes. After all,
I was going to the house of my King.
Quiet reigned in the sanctuary as I

103

entered. I sat in a pew and prayed like the other worshippers until the service began.

Now casual clothes are the norm. Summer means bare feet in sandals, shorts, and tube tops. In winter, it's jeans and sweaters with wild words on tees.

"We want to draw the young people," the worship committee explains.

No need to be reverent when you enter church either. No longer is it called a sanctuary, just an auditorium in a building. We're there to meet God, yes, but also friends, so "good to see you," fills the air. Gradually, I've adapted. My voice can also be heard. Sometimes I want to slap myself as I remember the old ways.

Changed too is our approach to worship songs. Gone are the

organ and piano. In their place are guitars, drums, and keyboard. The choir has been replaced with six or seven men and women on a platform wearing the above mentioned casual clothes. Another change from the day Mom Van Liere almost had a heart attack when the men marched into the choir loft wearing—not white—but colored dress shirts. Oh, and gone too, the hymn books. Now movie clips, Powerpoint, and projectors lead us along in song and worship.

Is this church? Doesn't God demand temples of cedar and beautiful stained glass cathedrals?

Lawrence O. Richards, in his book *Bible Teacher's' Commentary*, writes: "The church is people. Not organizations or buildings or programs, but people."

The ideas I grew up with have

fallen out of favor, but we're making new ones each Sunday. In the years to come, our new worship experience will probably seem antiquated and obsolete to the generations that follow. At the moment, we tend to see only what we have been accustomed to. Changes feel like an affront to what is proper.

I may have lost what I thought was the House of God, but I have found something new: A Lord who is at home in whatever "building" his followers gather—even a restaurant, a strip mall, or a retreat center on the side of a mountain trail.

Regardless of where we worship, we can meet our Lord in reverence, for it is not we who make a place holy but God.

Prayer

Most Holy God, I would kneel before You in reverence for You are so worthy. Thank You for saving me, for giving me life eternal. In the name of Jesus who made this possible, Amen.

A Step Further

Psalm 5:7; I Corinthians 6:19, 20; II Corinthians 6:16

Building Blocks of Faith

Where and how we worship matters less than who we worship.

Questions

If you knew God was seated on the pew next to you, would your posture change? What does it mean to be reverent?

The Neighborhood Project

Pure and undefiled religion before
God and the Father is this:
to visit orphans and widows
in their trouble.
James 1:27a (NKJ)

"My arthritis is getting to me,"
Jane said. "I can't care for the
house and yard as I used to do."

She was not complaining, just
stating a fact. A daughter and her
husband live in Alaska. They visit
three times a year and do what they
can to help tidy up Jane's home.
The last time they came they tossed
out her soaker-hose—the one with
all the tiny holes in it. They thought

it was ruined since soaker-hoses are unknown in the cold country.

"Since I can't take care of things the way I used to," Jane said with a grin, "I call myself the neighborhood project. This summer a neighbor saw me struggling with the shrubs in front of the house. He walked over. 'Here,' he said. 'I'll do that for you.'"

"This past winter, I was shoveling snow from my driveway. A couple and their young son stopped, took the shovel from my hands, and each took a turn clearing away the snow. When they were finished, the father gave me his card and said, 'Call us when you need us.' Who says there are no nice people in the world?"

If Jane is a neighborhood project, I must be my family's personal mission project. My daughter and grandson live with me. Between the two of them they mow the yard, trim the rose bushes, and do the weeding during the summer. In winter they shovel the driveway and put down ice-melt so I won't fall. I do the inside chores, like dusting and vacuuming. What a blessing it is to have someone else doing the heavy work.

And isn't that what James called pure religion? Aren't we commanded to visit the shut-ins, orphans, and widows? To feed the hungry, comfort the lonely, and meet the needs of those we can with the blessings and comfort we ourselves have received from others?

In the Kingdom of God we are all projects in need of repair and care. Today, find a shovel, broom, or hammer that fits your hand and get to work "projecting" His love.

Prayer

God, my Helper, thank You for sending all those who help us as we grow older. Bless them I pray. For the times I've taken that help for granted, forgive me. In the name of Jesus, I pray. Amen.

A Step Further

Psalm 65:24; Jeremiah 29:11, 12

Building Blocks of Faith

"Preach the Gospel at all times, use words when necessary."
Mother Teresa

Questions

What can I do for others? Is it hard for me to accept help?

Name Calling

Rise in the presence of the aged, show respect for the elderly and revere your God. I am the Lord.
Leviticus 19:32 (NIV)

Day one: "Here's your change, dearie. Thanks for shopping with us and have a good day." The cashier in City Market, about forty-five-years-old, handed me my change.

Day two: "Can I help you find something, honey?" A store clerk in her thirties offered to help me locate whatever I was hunting for in the newly redone, doubled-in-size department store.

"All I want to find is the front door,"

I said.

Day three: "Sign this for me, sweetie." The bank cashier pushed a slip across the counter for me to sign.

Sweetie? I have bunions on my feet older than she is, I thought.

How should I feel when others sweetly call me names? Should I frown at the familiarity? Look haughty? Smile politely? Or maybe I should say, with a touch of sarcasm, "Thanks darling—no, dearie—you got it, babe."

Yesterday a young woman in her late teens bagged my groceries in the checkout lane and placed them in my cart. As I started for the door she said, "Have a good day, ma'am."

I stopped and turned. "Ma'am? Wow, I like that."

She laughed. "Another lady almost bit my head off when I called her ma'am. She said she wasn't old enough to be called ma'am." The girl shrugged. "My Dad was in the military. We had to call women ma'am and men sir."

Am I making a big deal out of a minor matter? The names I've been called were not meant to be offensive, but they leave me feeling patronized. Yet, we take the same tone with God each time we informally address Him as pop, pal, and the old man upstairs. God has given us His names: Almighty, All-Sufficient, Master, and Lord. He is the Lord who provides, heals, and sanctifies. If I am offended when others address me with such informality, is God?

It seems I took the verse from Leviticus and twisted it until it turned and bit me. The next time someone calls me dearie, honey, or sweetie, I hope I'll accept their gesture for what it is; an acknowledgment that they noticed me and showed respect.

Prayer

Dear God. I'm embarrassed when I behave like a child. I'm old enough to start acting mature. Forgive me for my pettiness and help me be as nice to others as they are to me. I pray in the name of Jesus, the one who is forever kind. Amen.

A Step Further

Proverbs 16:24; I Thessalonians 5:15

Dare To Live

Building Blocks of Faith

Happy is the heart that forgives an offense.

Questions

Have I offended anyone today? How can I look past supposed insults and see the meaning behind the words?

117

Elizabeth Van Liere

Wandering Sheep

Suppose one of you has a hundred sheep and lost one. Wouldn't you leave the ninety-nine in the wilderness and go after the lost one until you found it?
Luke 15:4 (The Message)

Dennis Jernigan, a singer and song-writer of contemporary Christian music, has a great testimony. On his CDs, and in person, he tells of how he led a homosexual lifestyle for several years. When he became a Christian, he left that life behind.

One of his tours took him to his hometown in Oklahoma. After the concert he met with a friend of his deceased grandmother. The lady said, "For years I prayed for you with your grandmother and a group of other ladies. We asked the Lord to guide you back to Him." She hugged him and said, "How happy your grandmother must be right now."

Even when it seemed he would never change, these ladies continued praying for Dennis. The prayers were answered and Dennis turned to the Lord. His music now gives joy and inspiration to people everywhere, not just for the blessed songs, but for his testimony of hope.

This testimony encourages me to keep praying, especially for some of my grandkids. Jesus tells us to seek the lost, gather the scattered, and restore to the fold those we love. We should allow our love to be evident, prayers fervent, and arms open.

Believing that, I prayed for several years for one granddaughter, unmarried, but living with her beloved. I even found the courage to tell her, "God does not approve, dear."

"Gran'ma, times have changed," she said.

"But God hasn't," I told her.

With joy and laughter, I attended my granddaughter's wedding a few years ago. Now God blesses their union. I pray they will build a marriage that honors God and their love for each other.

But if they do not, I'll pray anyway. I can almost hear Dennis' grandmother saying, "Yes! Do! Prayer works."

God has given grandparents a special job: To pray for our kids, grandkids, great-grandkids, and beyond. Our family members are never out of sight when God is looking down on them. Precious souls, God wants them all.

Prayer

Lover of the children, help me to be faithful in praying for these, my children and yours. With all my heart I want to see them in heaven some day, but I know You love them even more than I do. Lead them into the knowledge of Jesus, Your Son who is waiting for them with open, loving arms. In His name I pray, Amen.

A Step Further

Mark 10:15, 16; James 5:19, 20; Ephesians 3:14-21

Building Blocks of Faith

Intercessory prayer: Social networking on a heavenly basis.

Questions

How serious am I about praying for my family? How much do I want to meet them in heaven?

A Different Direction

A man can do nothing better than to eat and drink and find satisfaction in his work. This too, I see, is from the hand of God, for without Him, who can eat or find enjoyment?
Ecclesiastes 2: 24, 25 (NIV)

Carla focused her life on caring for her husband and two children. Not just cooking and cleaning, but taking time to nurture her youngsters spiritually. She explained one way she did this.

"Jack and I took time to run the Bible Bowl," she said. "We taught memory verses from the Bible, not just to our children, but to others as well. Kids from other states slept overnight when they came for competitions. And oh, the van loads of noisy kids we took when other churches held competitions."

Carla's children have grown up. Now she and Jack find enjoyment in their two grandchildren. Since Jack's retirement they have time for themselves, but serving is still an important part of Carla's life. Recently, she found something pulling her into a new and different direction. She became a member of our city council. "It's another way of serving," she says.

I, too, cared for my family in many of the same ways and when I pictured retirement, I never imagined myself sitting in a rocking chair and knitting a shawl for someone in the hospital. First off, rocking makes me dizzy and, second, my knitting leaves too many extra holes. Will you find me at the local senior center playing cards? Nope. Too boring. Run for a public position? Are you kidding me?

No, if you want to find me serving others you'll find my shoes parked under my desk with me seated at my computer. I'm free to think, type, and turn out what I hope is an article, devotion, or poem that will turn someone's thoughts to God. We're all called to serve in different ways. Carla serves in public ways. I serve in solitude. But both our efforts find a larger audience beyond the bounds of our homes.

Each of us is unique. God has some kind of service each of us can fulfill, no matter how young or old we are. To find satisfaction in your labor is a blessing from God, be it in knitting, writing, or running for office. The key is to be at work for Him no matter what your age.

Somewhere at this very moment, someone is in need of your talents. Get to work.

Prayer

Giver of all good gifts, I thank You for letting me share Your love through the joy of writing. You touched my heart for others and with Your help I can help them see You. For Jesus' sake and in His name, I pray, Amen.

A Step Further

Psalm 92:12-15; Proverbs 20:24

Building Blocks of Faith

We develop spiritual muscles by serving others through Christ.

Questions

Have I let my age settle me into old age before my time? How can I serve Him best?

Elizabeth Van Liere

Words As Weapons

Let the words of my mouth and
the meditation of my heart. Be
acceptable in Your sight, O Lord,
my rock and my Redeemer.
Psalm 19:14 (NAS)

It's a bad habit. I pop off remarks
that seem cute when I say them.
Everyone laughs, including the
person about whom the funny dig
is made. But afterward, the sight
of the person I zinged is haunting.
She's no longer laughing, just sitting
silently and I feel nasty.

All humor must have a target.
When we laugh at others we are
secretly congratulating ourselves
that someone else is the object of

ridicule, not us. We may think we're being clever or cute, when really we are cruel and cutting.

My husband also had a similar "verbal filter" problem. On a trip to Costa Rica, as we waited for our meal in a nice restaurant, a couple of young American men came in. Their clothes were dirty. Their long hair needed washing. Their rather flirtatious behavior with the waitress left me wondering about their morals. I hope this isn't what others think of Americans, I thought.

My husband evidently felt the same. He remarked, in his usual loud tone, "Rich kids. Their dad is probably paying for them to hang out down here."

A few minutes later, one of the men said rather loudly to the waitress, "I'm pooped. Just got back from working the docks. What's good, honey? The usual?"

Needless to say, neither my husband nor I said another word. We choked our meal down and sneaked out of the restaurant without looking back.

Come to think of it, maybe I caught the habit of speaking without thinking from my husband. Oops . . . there I go again. I know, I know. We are each responsible for our own insensitive words.

A sage once said, "What you are when you are young only intensifies as you grow older." If that's true, I hope I was nicer in my youth than I am now. I want my niceness to grow stronger, not my nastiness.

It's just as easy to say kind things as hurtful ones. Besides, it's what Jesus wants.

Prayer

Kind and merciful Father, help me think before I say another hurtful word. I ask this in the name of Jesus, whose every thought and word were love. In His name I pray, Amen.

A Step Further

Proverbs 25:11; Matthew 12:36, 37

Building Blocks of Faith

God not only sees us, He hears each word we speak.

Questions

When people laugh because I say something cutting, does it glorify God? How do you feel when you are the object of a joke?

We're Right, They're Wrong

Now I exhort you, brethren, by the name of our Lord Jesus Christ, that you all agree and that there be no divisions among you, but that you be made complete in the same mind and in the same judgment.
I Corinthians 1:10 (NAS)

Fingerswerepointed.Accusations made. Result: About fifty seniors left our church and started a new one. They were hurt by words and actions. Those who stayed, like me, knew only bits and pieces about what happened.

I spoke to two of our ministers and heard their side of the story. From those who left I heard another side. Undoubtedly both sides had a fault in the matter. Each side said, "We're right. They're wrong."

The judgment didn't stop there. It cut between individuals. One of my friends in the new church said, "Nobody thinks less of you for not coming with us."

Immediately my defenses rose. "Why should they?" I exclaimed. "I don't judge any of you for leaving. This church is right for me. The minister preaches the Word. I have lots of friends here." One by one my reasons assailed her as though I was hitting baseballs in a batting cage.

When two people or two parties disagree, the reason may be serious or silly, but the result is division within the Body of Christ, separating even friends.

In writing to the church in Corinth, Paul encouraged his friends to agree—not on sermon content, music tastes, or matters of mission, budget or buildings—but on divisions within the church. "Agree that there be no divisions among you."

Like a cancer cell, the disease of disharmony divides and multiples within the Body of Christ until the Church becomes sick and weak.

Those who left our congregation remain my friends, just as the ones who stayed are also my friends. When an illness or death or hardship strikes any of them, I pray for them, as I hope they pray for me.

Who was wrong in our church? Who was wrong in my friend's words and my defensive attitude? Jon Brown, a pastor in Washington says, "… Christian unity is more than just reaching agreement. It comes only when we are willing to put others before ourselves." I pray God will give me the grace to accept those with whom I disagree and to not just tolerate them, but love them as Christ loves me.

Prayer

Father of all wisdom, look down on me and give me a willing heart; a heart that wants to put others before herself, not one who too often says, "I'm right. And that's the end of it." Give me an ear to hear the other person's side. In the name of Jesus, Amen.

A Step Further

Romans 16:17; Titus 3:9

Building Blocks of Faith

The antidote of discord is grace.

Questions

When was the last time you listened to another's opinion... and changed your mind?

Come and See

Nathanael said, "Nazareth! You've got to be kidding." But Philip said, "Come, see for yourself."
John 1:46 (The Message)

"The older I get the more I want to see Jesus," Betty Jo said in one of our Bible studies.

She had been ill for a year or more. Unexplained aches and pains. Unable to sleep at night and dozing off during the day. Doctor appointments. New medications. Nothing helped. Did it discourage her? No. It just increased her longing to see Jesus.

This man from Nazareth has a

137

strange way of showing us what is good. During my friend's slow, painful ascent towards heaven, the main thing on her mind was not her undiagnosed illness. Her main focus was on the day she would see Jesus.

She focused her prayers on other things too: An unbelieving son-in-law whom she hoped would come to know the Savior, her unmarried grandson living with his sweetheart, and healing for a daughter suffering with MS. All mattered deeply to her. Her goal was they too would "come and see" Jesus.

Jesus Himself told two of John the Baptist's disciples to "come and see" when they came to Him and asked, "Teacher, where are you staying?" They followed and found not just a good man or great teacher, but God Himself.

One of the two who followed

Jesus that day was Andrew. The first thing he did was bring his brother, Simon Peter, to Jesus. Then Philip, like Andrew, told Nathanael about Jesus. Until Nathanael met Jesus himself, he thought Phillip was speaking foolishly when he said he'd found something good in Nazareth—just as others think we are irrational in our devotion to a Savior we can't see, touch, or smell.

"Come and see," Jesus says. Like my friend, I long to see the throne of Christ. I wait for the day when I can bow at His feet and touch for myself the nail holes that made me whole.

"Come and see what I have found," said Phillip.

Won't you come with me?

Prayer

My God, You have given me a long life and extra time to tell others about You. Let the words "come and see" ring loudly in my heart and mouth. For the sake of my Savior, Jesus, Amen.

A Step Further

John 4:28-30, 39; Revelation 22:12

Building Blocks of Faith

God's ways are not our ways but they work anyway.

Questions

List the ways you know Christ is real and ask: "Am I content to simply *know* Jesus or am I telling others to 'Come and see?'"

What Am I Missing Here?

Whatever is good and perfect comes to us from God above, who created all heaven's lights. Unlike them he never changes or casts shlfting shadows.
James 1:17 (NLT)

"No, I don't think I'll go. I'll stay home. I'm kinda tired."

"Oh, come on, Mom," my daughter said. "We'll take a lawn chair and you can sit while the rest of us hike up the river."

She won. I settled in the back seat with my three-year-old great granddaughter in her car seat next to me. Forty-five minutes later we turned down the gravel road into the Silver Jack recreation area. Bumpy and rough, the road wound past pastures, next to a creek, and then through a forested area.

Miles farther we pulled off the road and parked next to the Cimarron River. My daughter set my chair up near the rushing stream. Spray bubbled up, sparkling in the sun. The noisy water made its own music as it tumbled over rocks.

Towering cliffs framed the soft blue sky that was filled with white billowy clouds. Tall green pines hugged the road, a hiding place for bear and deer and other forest creatures.

My family left me there while they hiked up stream. I sat and looked and filled my eyes and heart with God's wonderful world, a place apart.

James reminds us to look to the giver of all things good and perfect and give him praise. For us to do that, however, we need to get out and look. We must leave the comfort of our couch, chair, and bed, and step into His creation. Though the mountains quake and the heavens shake, God never changes. He's the same today as he was yesterday and will be tomorrow.

As we grow older it becomes easier to say, "No, I'll just stay home." The effort of rising and leaving weighs upon us. Who knows how many special moments with God I may have missed because I hunkered down in my easy chair and read—or dozed. Missed moments to look and see beyond the problems our sad world is facing. Missed moments to see what God intended when He created the beauty that is ours for the taking. Missed precious moments to hold in my heart for a day when I'm unable to leave my home or bed.

Christ came that we might have life and have it to the full. We can't savor all He has created if we don't drink deeply from the wellspring of life. Make it your goal to accept each day as a gift from God and savor every moment.

Prayer

Heavenly Creator, I thank You for the times You've given me. Special moments that restore my soul. Give me the wisdom to get out of my lazy chair, to "get up and go" when I have the chance, ready to behold the beauty You have created, showing me there is more than ugliness in the world today. Because of Jesus, Your co-creator, Amen.

A Step Further

Genesis 1:31; Revelation 22:1-5

Building Blocks of Faith

Faith believes something will happen before it does.

Questions

Do I use my age as an excuse to ignore God's blessings? Can I find a painting more beautiful than what God has painted?

One Man's Junk is Another Man's Treasure

For where your treasure is, there will
your heart be also.
Matthew 6:21(KJ)

Yard Sale. Come one, come all.
You'll surely find something you
can't live without.

For months, I've been saying,
"I've got to get rid of stuff." Stuff
like books by some of my favorite
authors, including Ken Gire, Calvin
Miller, and Madeline L'Engle. There
is a catch, however. These books
can only go to someone who will
treasure them as I do.

How about the fifty plus "How

to Write" books? I'll make you a special deal on them right now. Clothes for all seasons? Look no further. A missing dish from your grandmother's china collection? I have it, I'm sure.

The trouble is, I don't *want* to get rid of my treasures. I hang onto things way too long, thinking I can use them again. They can't be *that* worn out.

For instance, I go to water aerobics twice a week and the chlorine in the water left my swimsuit faded. To say it's hanging on by the last thread would be a compliment. This summer at J. C. Penny I bought a colorful replacement at a great price. Then I thought, Oh, dear. The chlorine will ruin this one, too. For several weeks I continued wearing the old one until it hit me: You aren't going swimming anywhere else, Elizabeth. Wear the new one.

Before I could regret it I tossed the other one in the trash.

Jesus said, "Where your treasure is, there your heart will be also." Actually, what are my treasures? The books I've read once and won't re-read? The out-dated clothes? One mismatched china dish out of a set? Who knows what treasures He would give me if only I would let go of the old and reach for the new.

Today I'm packing up my beloved dust catchers, dishes, and rocks. (Yes, rocks. My husband and I were rock hounds and I have some beauties.) Each knickknack is a souvenir from the past that brings memories of special moments. Will anyone want them? Doesn't matter. I'm letting them go.

These things were once my treasures, but when I leave for heaven they'll become what they already are to others—junk—the evidence of a cluttered life. These possessions hold memories but they can't hold me. My real treasure is His word, which is hidden in my heart. The rest lies not in the past but the future, in heaven, to which I'm going. It's not a collectible, but a person. Someone called Jesus.

God gave me days on earth to enjoy, treasures to cherish like trips with my family, and souvenirs of special times. But all these things were and are, temporary. They will pass… as will I.

While everything else disappears, Jesus remains.

Prayer

Father, giver of good gifts, I thank you for all You have given me, from the smallest—a piece of Your creation—a rock, to the biggest—knowing Jesus loves me. Help me share this love, for no matter how often I share it, I still have plenty more. In His precious name I pray, Amen.

A Step Further

Psalm 84:11; Isaiah 33:6

Building Blocks of Faith

Take stock of your eternal treasures and give thanks.

Questions

Is Jesus the most treasured possession in your life? If not, why not? List five people you fear are lost. Will you share this treasured possession with them?

Blessed Hope

But those who hope in the Lord will renew their strength, They will soar on wings like eagles, they will run and not grow weary, they will walk and not be faint.
Isaiah 40:31 (NIV)

Heartbreak struck our family when my grandson, David, was nine. A car hit him, changing him from an always-running, always-shouting, always-happy boy to an inactive child, with tubes keeping him alive.

David turned thirty-six a few days ago. He lies on his hospital bed in the living room, the center of family activity. The tubes are gone, except for the one in his stomach. Through that tube, his body receives the nourishment it needs, for he cannot swallow. Neither can he speak or move. From his bed he is lifted daily to his wheel chair by a Hoyer lift.

The biggest share of caring for David rests with his loving parents. My daughter-in-law bathes him, dresses and feeds him with the aid of a helper. His dad, my son, feeds him first thing in the morning before he goes to work. He talks to him and makes him smile.

Where they go, David goes. Churchgoers greet him. "Hey, David. How's it going?" They are rewarded with a lopsided smile.

On weekend trips when staying at a motel, his dad says, "Ready for a swim, David?" Into the pool they go.

While his sisters were growing up, the first thing they did when they came home from school was run to him and say, "Hi, David," and give him a hug.

On my yearly visit, I hold his hand, kiss him and say, "Good to see you, honey." A welcoming smile crosses his face. It tells me, "I'm so glad to see you, Gran'ma." When I leave to return home, his blank look says, "I wish you could stay."

David's patient family knows he is locked inside himself, waiting for the day the promise from Isaiah comes true. All of us believe *he will walk again in heaven.*

This is the motto my kids live by— one that has carried them all these years—one we can all embroider on our hearts: *As long as we keep our eyes on Jesus, we are okay.*

Prayer

Heavenly Father, I see the great witness for You to the world in the way my kids care for David. I believe the words of Isaiah will someday be fulfilled for David. Thank You for this blessed hope, made possible by Your Son, Jesus. Amen.

A Step Further

Psalm 84:6, 7; Romans 5:3-5

Building Blocks of Faith

Even in the darkness the light of Jesus shines brightly.

Questions

Am I keeping my eyes on Jesus at all times?

I Was Here

…I will not forget you. See, I have inscribed you on the palms of my hands.
Isaiah 49:15b (NKJ)

We stopped for lunch at a roadside park where dunes spilled sand beneath the picnic table. We ate sandy sandwiches and drank grit-flavored lemonade. We watched five giggly girls and four rambunctious boys as they climbed, rolled, and stomped their names in four-foot letters on the sand slopes.

One boy worked his name with neater letters, six feet high instead of four. Deeply imprinted was the name AARON.

"Okay, kids. Let's go," the youth director shouted.

Screams and yells funneled back into the waiting cars. Seventy-five miles down the road my husband and I left the group setting up camp at the lake. We had volunteered "transportation only" to and from a youth weekend campout. Leaving the chaperoning, refereeing, and pacifying in younger hands, we went on a twenty-four-hour rock hunting expedition.

We returned the next day, rested and restored, ready to tackle the trip home. But where was the tent village? No noisy kids greeted us. No tired adults sighed in relief to see us. "Do you suppose someone got sick?" I said.

We circled the campground, then stopped at the ranger station.

"Hope nothing's wrong," my husband said. "I'll see if there's a message.'

When he returned, his face was as white as the note he handed me. Thirty minutes after we left, Aaron had drowned. This was in the days before cell phones so other church members had been called from the park to come for the youngsters.

We started back on a highway stretching forever, the two of us and one other passenger. A passenger called silence.

We passed the picnic area where the sand was still drifting. All names but one had been blown away. The wind had just begun erasing AARON, like a teacher reluctant to erase yesterday's lesson.

AARON. My name is AARON, and I was here.

It happened forty years ago, but Aaron's story still lives in my heart. None of us want to be forgotten after we die. God assures us, *He* will never forget us. He loves us and when we accept His love through Jesus, we will meet Him one day in heaven.

Prayer

Father of us all, I am now almost eight times older than Aaron was so long ago. The wind has long covered the place where he printed his name. I thank You that no winds can erase my name from Your memory. I thank You for Your promise to remember me. I know it is because You love me. In Jesus' name, Amen.

Elizabeth Van Liere

A Step Further

Isaiah 46:4; John 17:6; I Peter 2:9, 10

Building Blocks of Faith

Remember God and He will
remember you.

Questions

Do I include God in my daily
life? Am I remembering God by
spending time with Him?

More Inspirational Books From
❋ Christian Devotions Books ❋
www.christiandevotionsbooks.com/

Answering the Call -
Inspirational Devotionals from a Tested Paramedic
by Pat Patterson   ***Price: $9.95***

Jesus said, "Greater love has no one than this, that he lay down his life for his friends." The First Responders in your community do just that. They sacrifice comfort and safety to protect the lives of others, always waiting, and always wondering when they will find themselves answering the next call. This book was written for them, but it applies to anyone who searches for courage and hope, struggles with a difficult relationship, or suffers through pain or loss. Are you seeking a closer walk with God? Wondering what comes next? Answering the Call can help you find your way. It reveals the simple truth that Jesus Christ is Lord, and that to follow him is to find true meaning in life. Christ... the First Responder, is calling you now.

Will you be answering the call? "The promise is for you and your children and for all who are far off -for all whom the Lord our God will call." - Acts 2:39.

Learn more about this book at: www.answeringthecall.us

Faith & FINANCES:
In God We Trust, A Journey to Financial Dependence
by Christian Devotions contributors   ***Price: $9.95***

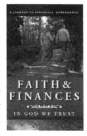

Jesus spoke about money and material possessions more than he talked about heaven, hell, or prayer. He noted the relationship between a man's heart and his wallet, warning, "Where your treasure is, there your heart will be." This contemporary retelling of the Rich Young Ruler brings a fresh look at the relationship between a person's faith and their finances. Within the pages of Faith & FINANCES: In God We Trust you'll find spiritual insight and practical advice from Christy award-winning writer Ann Tatlock, plus best-selling authors, Loree Lough, Yvonne Lehman, Virginia Smith, Irene Brand, DiAnn Mills, Miralee Ferrell, Shelby Rawson and many more.

Great faith calls us to trust God, not our wealth. Read how others have cast off the golden handcuffs and learned to live the abundant life Jesus promised in this contemporary retelling of the Rich Young Ruler. Faith & FINANCES: In God We Trust, A Journey to Financial Dependence - turning the hearts of a nation back toward God one paycheck at a time.

Learn more about this book at: www.faithandfinances.us

Spirit & HEART: A Devotional Journey
by Christian Devotions contributors   Price: $9.95

What is a devotional journey? It is the Bible. Today we enjoy the benefit of the prayers, wisdom, praise and sorrow of people who, during their lifetime, chose to remember the times God worked in their lives. That is devotion to God and dedication to recording "His Story." The daily devotions included in this book are heartfelt stories, lessons, and advice from others who have traveled the devotional journey. This book is a primer, a tool to get you started on the path toward spending your best moments with the Father. Christ says, where your heart is there your treasure will be. Treasure His words and whispers as you walk in the footsteps of award-winning authors Ann Tatlock, Loree Lough, Yvonne Lehman, Virginia Smith, Irene Brand, Shelby Rawson, Eddie Jones, Cindy Sproles, Ariel Allison-plus many more.

Learn more about this book at: www.devotionsbook.com

Emerson The Magnificent!
by Dwight Ritter   Price: $12.99

"A charming little book for young and old."

How an old bike takes a young man for the ride of his life.

"What a delight... though I thought it unlikely that a bicycle could do much to unravel some complicated issues, my skepticism was outvoted. It really doesn't matter how old you are, Emerson talks to you. Dwight Ritter's illustrations made me smile as much as his story warmed my heart. Emerson's message challenged my thinking, then threw me a lifeline, reeled me in and rescued me. Get it! Read it! Give it to everyone you know! " - by Pat Lindquist.

Learn more about this book at: www.emersonthemagnificent.com

Open Your Hymnal -
Devotions That Harmonize Scripture With Song
by Denise K. Loock   Price: $9.95

Do you ever catch yourself singing a song in church without paying attention to the words? Open Your Hymnal is a collection of thirty meditations that transport the wisdom of classic hymns and gospel songs into the twenty-first century. Introduce yourself to the rich spiritual heritage that hymnals contain or gain a new perspective on songs you've sung since childhood. Whether you sing in the choir loft, the worship team, or the pew, the refreshing biblical insights in this book will enhance your appreciation of the words you sing every time you open a hymnal.

Learn more about this book at www.digdeeperdevotions.com/books.aspx

**More Inspirational Books Available From
Christian Devotions Ministry's Book Division
www.christiandevotionsbooks.com**

2011 Releases

He Said, She Said: A Devotional Guide to Cultivating a Life of Passion, *or How Newlyweds, Couples and Singles Can Draw Closer to God and Their Mate Through Daily Devotions*

by Eddie Jones, Cindy Sproles
Price: $9.95

Do you sense something vital missing from your relationship with your spouse, children and God? Are you easily distracted by the busyness of life and left feeling drained, bored, and discouraged? Do you sense you were meant to enjoy the richness of life, but spend your days feasting on crumbs? This heart-warming collection of stories (54 in all) will inspire you to reach for the true source of joy: a life lived for and through God. These deeply personal (and sometimes humorous) devotions offer biblical insights and spiritual truths from the unique perspective of one man and one woman. Learn to cultivate a life of passion. Perfect for your quiet time, these moments of meditative reflection illustrate the importance of allowing God to work within you and speak through you. No matter if you are newlyweds or newly retired, this book of devotions will help you put the spark back into your love life and explore the precious relationships God desires for you. He Said, She Said touches the heart, tickles the funny bone and brings you to your knees in worship.

Dare to Live: Devotions for Those Over The Hill, Not Under It!

by Elizabeth Van Liere   *Price: $9.95*

Dare to Live: Devotions for Those Over The Hill, Not Under It! is a jolt of spiritual inspiration, a quick boost for your soul. Rediscover God's grace, hope, and power for living-regardless of your place or age in life. In Dare to Live 87-year-old author Elizabeth Van Liere leads readers through a thirty-day journey to a fuller understanding of what it means to "season slowly with a mighty and loving Savior." This journey pursues a life characterized by relevancy not regret, generosity not grumpiness, and compassion to the end. These quick shots of instant inspiration might be just what you need to keep going. Whether new to the faith or a life-long follower of Christ, readers old and young will discover the joy of what it means to be transformed into the image of Jesus and used for His purposes to the very end. The perfect companion for those Over The Hill, Not Under It! Start living for Him, now!

38293682R00102

Made in the USA
Columbia, SC
04 December 2018